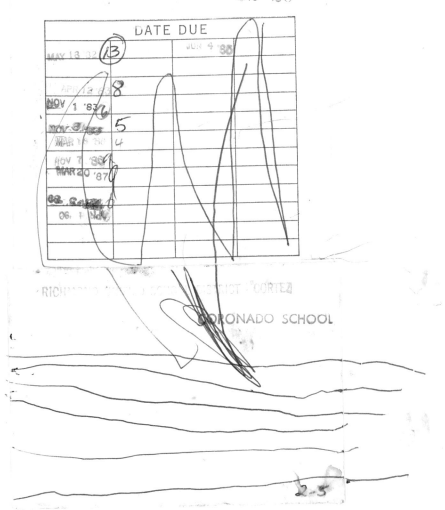

WHALES

Thanks are due to the following for kind
permission to reproduce photographs:
Greenpeace Movement; Barbara Lipton; British
Natural History Museum; Novosti Press Agency;
Radio Times Hulton Picture Library; Sea Mammal
Research Unit; United States Travel Service

R.L. 2.9 Spache Revised Formula

Library of Congress Cataloging in Publication Data

Harris, Susan.
  Whales.

  (An Easy-read fact book)
  Includes index.
  SUMMARY: Describes the physical
characteristics and habits of various types of whales.
    1. Whales—Juvenile literature. [1.Whales] I. Chan-
nell, Jim. II. Title.
QL737.C4H3   599'.5   79-13276
ISBN 0-531-00444-9

6 5 4 3 2 1

WHALES

SUSAN HARRIS

Illustrated by Jim Channell

AN EASY-READ FACT BOOK

FRANKLIN WATTS
New York/London/Toronto/Sydney/1980

Whales look like very large fish. In fact, they used to be called **"whale-fish."** But whales are not fish at all. Whales are **mammals.** So are humans, apes, and mice.

Main differences between whales and fish

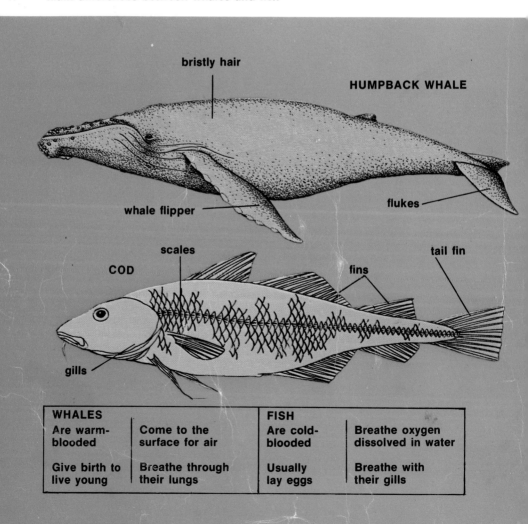

bristly hair

HUMPBACK WHALE

whale flipper

flukes

scales

tail fin

COD

fins

gills

WHALES		FISH	
Are warm-blooded	Come to the surface for air	Are cold-blooded	Breathe oxygen dissolved in water
Give birth to live young	Breathe through their lungs	Usually lay eggs	Breathe with their gills

Bottlenosed dolphin giving birth

Mammals give birth to live young. They have **lungs** to breathe with. The **body temperature** of mammals always stays the same. The weather or season does not change their temperature. Most mammals have some **hair** on their bodies. Whales are the only mammals that always live in water.

There are about 100 different **species** (kinds) of whales. They include **dolphins, killer whales,** and **blue whales.** The blue whale is the largest of all. In fact, blue whales are the largest animals that have ever lived. Blue whales are even bigger than the **dinosaur** was.

Model of a dinosaur

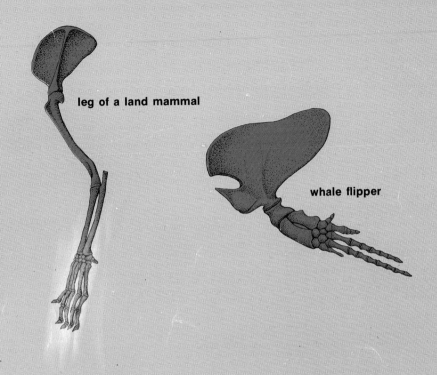

leg of a land mammal

whale flipper

Scientists call this group of mammals cetaceans (se-TA-shens). Millions of years ago, cetaceans were probably land animals. Land animals have four legs. Over millions of years, two of the cetacean's legs gradually disappeared. The other two evolved (changed) into flippers or fins. And so whales are now sea mammals.

Other mammals have hair to protect them from the cold. Most whales have little or no hair. Instead, they have a **thick** layer of **fat.** It is called **blubber.** The blubber is right under their skin.

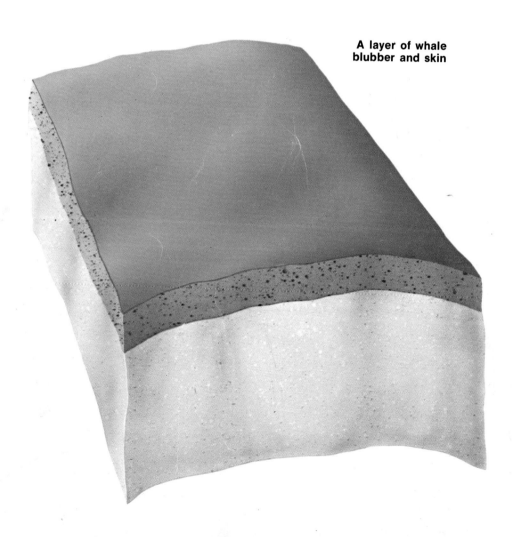

A layer of whale blubber and skin

Pilot whales live part of the year in cold waters.

Blubber helps keep **heat** in the body. Rather like woolen clothes on a cold day. Blubber is also a **store** of food. Whales sometimes need this when they can't find food. They swim long distances from cold to warm waters. These long swims, or **journeys,** are called **migrations** (my-GRAY-shins).

How are these **enormous** (e-NOR-muss) heavy creatures able to float? First, the layer of blubber is **lighter than water.** Second, they have large amounts of air in their lungs. Air is also lighter than water. Together, these things make the whale **buoyant** (keep it afloat).

Right whale

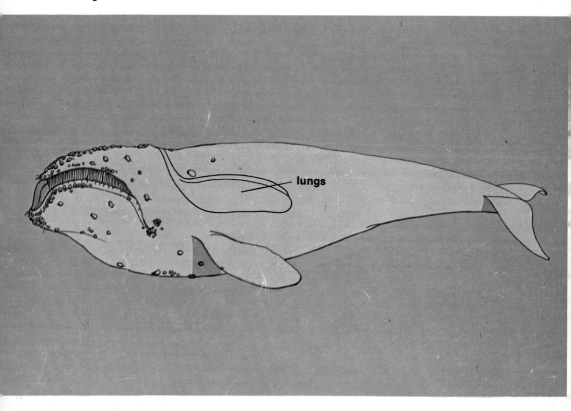

lungs

Minke whale

A whale's body is **streamlined** (has a smooth form). The head, body, and tail are one long shape. This allows the whale to move quickly and easily through water.

A whale's powerful tail ends in two **fleshy flukes.** The flukes lie flat in the water. They move and steer the whale. Just like the **propeller** and **rudder** of a ship. On each side of the body is a flipper, or fin. These two flippers help to steer and balance. Most whales also have a **dorsal** (back) fin. This is on top of the body.

Tail flukes of whales

blowhole

Dolphin breathing through its blowhole

Whales need air to breathe. But they can stay **underwater** for long periods. They breathe through nostrils, called **blowholes.** They have one or two blowholes on top of their head. A whale can open its mouth underwater. This is because it breathes only through the blowholes.

Before a whale **dives,** it **surfaces** several times. Each time it breathes in air. Between breaths it goes just below the water surface. When its lungs are full of air, the blowhole closes. Then the whale can dive deep under the sea.

Right whale about to dive

Most whales usually dive about 100 to 200 feet (30 to 60 m) down. **Sperm whales** are **champion** divers. They can stay underwater for up to 90 minutes. Sperm whales can dive to a depth of more than 360 feet (110 m).

Sperm whale diving

After a dive a whale must surface. The blowhole comes to the top first. Then the whale breathes out. A white spray, or **spout,** goes high into the air. The spout looks like a **fountain.** Different types of whales have different kinds of spouts.

Blue whale spout

Gray whale spout

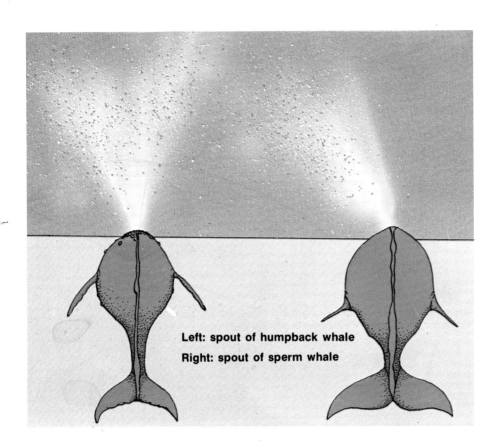

Left: spout of humpback whale
Right: spout of sperm whale

The blue whale has a high, straight spout. It may rise 18 to 30 feet (5 to 9 m) into the air. A **sperm whale's** spout goes up over its left side. The **humpback whale** has a high, unevenly-shaped spout. The **Greenland right whale** has two blowholes. So it has a V-shaped spout.

People who hunt whales are called **whalers.**
When whalers see a spout, they say the whale is
blowing. They can tell what kind of whale it is from
the shape of the spout. Whales must breathe out
when they surface. Most scientists think the spout
is their warm breath mixed with water droplets.

Whaling ship of the 1900's. As the whale "blows," a
harpoon is fired from a specially built gun.

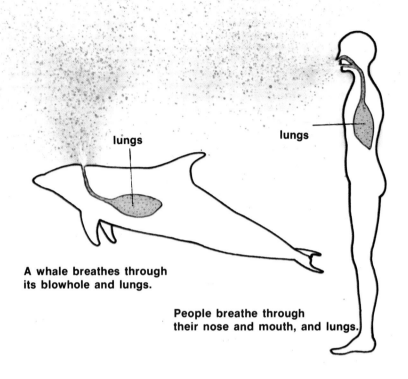

lungs

lungs

A whale breathes through its blowhole and lungs.

People breathe through their nose and mouth, and lungs.

Warm air **condenses** (steams) when it meets **cooler** air. That's what happens on a cold day when you can see your breath. Other scientists think the spout is small droplets of oil and **mucus** (MEW-kus). Mucus is a slimy (SLY-me) substance found in whales' lungs.

All animals need **information** about their surroundings. They need this in order to **survive** (sir-VIVE). They must know where to find food. And when to avoid danger.

Female humpback whale protecting her young

Whales learn about the underwater world mainly by **listening.** Ears are their most important **sensory** (SEN-sore-e) organ. It is difficult to see a whale's ears. That's because the outer ears are only very small slits. And the inner ear doesn't show at all.

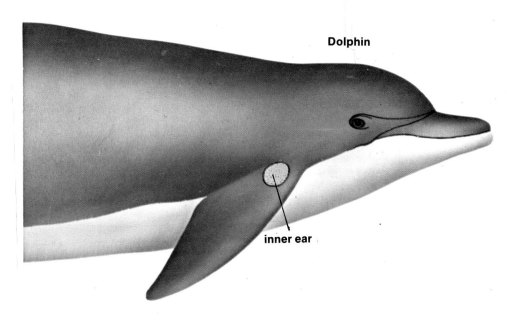

Dolphin

inner ear

A whale uses its ears to listen for enemies. And it listens for the calls of other whales.

Whales make a number of different sounds. They may **grunt, creak, whistle,** or **trill.** Dolphins make a **high-pitched** whistling noise. **White,** or **beluga** (be-LOO-ga) whales seem to sing. White whales are sometimes called "sea canaries."

White (beluga) whale

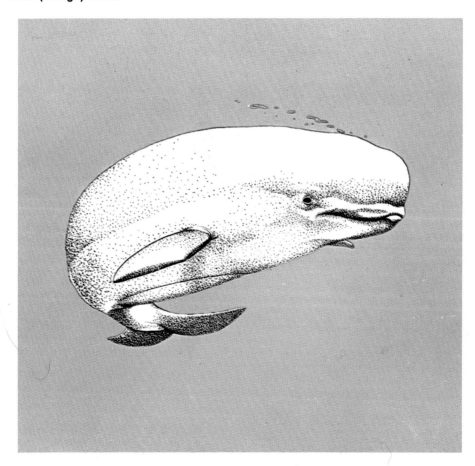

Many sounds that whales make are very high-pitched. The human ear is not able to hear them. Whales use these sounds to speak with each other. They also use sound to locate objects in the water.

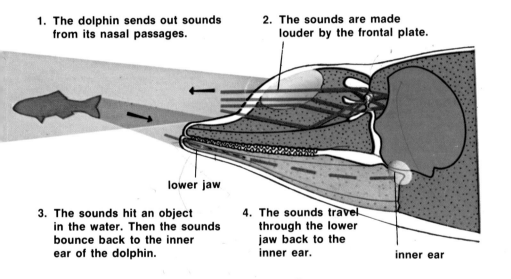

1. The dolphin sends out sounds from its nasal passages.

2. The sounds are made louder by the frontal plate.

lower jaw

3. The sounds hit an object in the water. Then the sounds bounce back to the inner ear of the dolphin.

4. The sounds travel through the lower jaw back to the inner ear.

inner ear

Finding things by using sound is called **echolocation,** or **sonar** (SO-nar).

There are two groups of whales: the **baleen** (ba-LEAN) whales and the **toothed** whales. The Greenland right whale and the **finback whale** are baleens. And so are the blue whale and the humpback whale. The humpback whale is about 40 feet (12 m) long. It weighs around 29 tons. The blue whale can grow up to 98 feet (30 m) long. And it can weigh about 130 tons. This is as much as a whole herd of elephants!

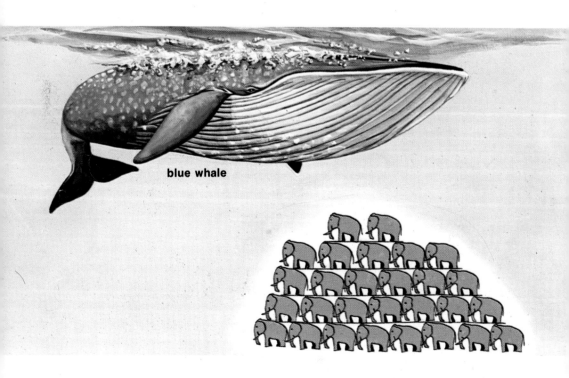

blue whale

Blue whales may be enormous. But they live on tiny animals called **krill.** Krill look like small shrimp. They are found near the surface of the sea. Krills stay together and cover the water in a reddish-brown **mass.** This mass may be three times bigger than a football field.

Krill—drawn approximately twice its actual size

Baleen whales do not have any teeth. Instead, they have long fringes of baleen, or **whalebone.** This hangs from the gums of the upper jaw. Baleen is made from **keratin** (KER-at-in). So is the human fingernail. Baleen whales feed by swimming with their mouths open.

Mouth of a finback whale, showing baleen

Every so often, the whale closes its mouth. The baleen traps the krill inside the whale's mouth. And the water flows out again into the sea. Using its tongue, the whale pushes the krill into its throat.

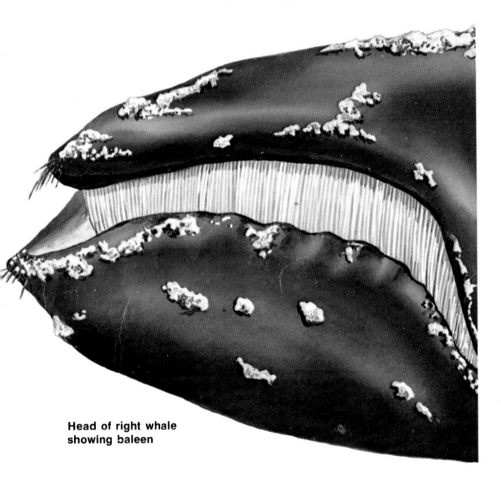

Head of right whale showing baleen

Blue whales may eat as much as 4 tons of krill in one day.

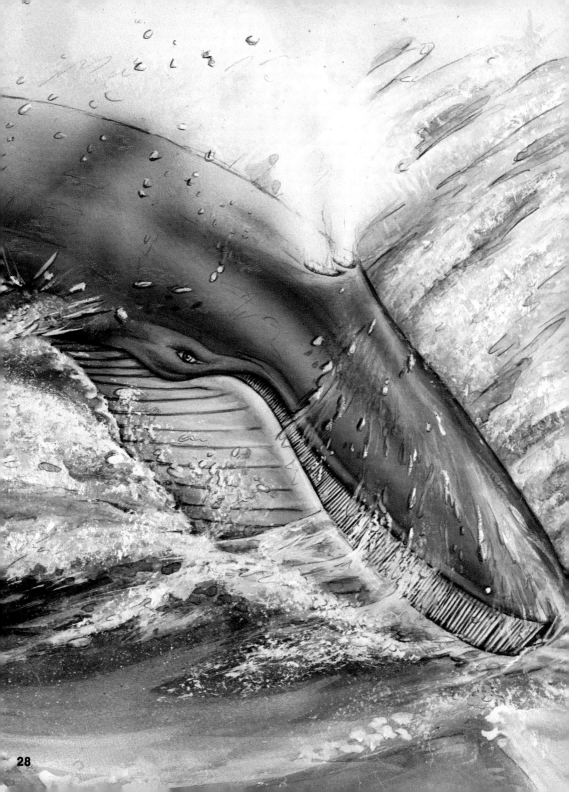

Krill are found in the **Arctic** (ARK-tik) and **Antarctic** (ant-ARK-tik) oceans. Baleen whales live in these areas during the summer. Before winter comes, they mate. Then they migrate (MY-grate) to warmer waters to give birth. Most baleen whales spend the winter near the equator (e-KWAT-or). From the cold seas to the tropical (TROP-e-kal) waters is about 2,670 miles (4,300 km). A whale takes about three months to swim this distance.

World map to show pattern of whale migration

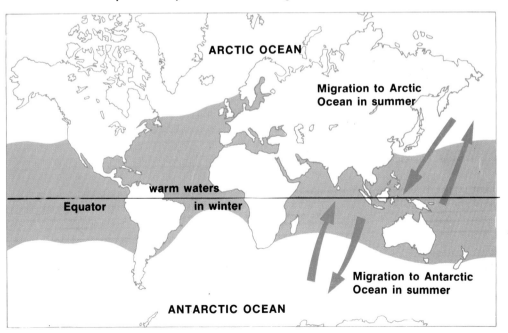

A newly-born whale has no protective layer of blubber. So warm water is the best place for a **calf** (baby whale) to be born. **Cows** (female whales) give birth to one calf every two years. For nearly one year the baby develops inside the mother's body. Then birth takes place underwater.

The mother must push her calf to the surface for its first breath. Soon its lungs are full of air. Now it is ready to swim beside its mother.

The calf gets food by drinking its mother's milk. It feeds on the creamy milk for about seven months. The cows guard their young constantly. There is always danger in the ocean.

Blue whale with calf.

A blue whale calf, the largest baby in the world, can weigh up to 2½ tons at birth.
Its weight doubles in a week.
The calf can drink 158 gallons (600 litres) of milk a day.

The other group of whales are the **toothed whales.** Toothed whales are **hunters.** They feed mainly on fish and **squid.** Much of their time is spent searching for food. Once the food is caught, it is usually swallowed whole. Or it may be crushed first by the whale's jaws or teeth. Whales do not use their teeth for chewing.

Head of killer whale

Some toothed whales have as many as 260 teeth. But the male **narwhal** has only two teeth. However, one tooth looks more like a **tusk** than a tooth. It sticks out for about 8 feet (2.5 m). No one knows for sure how the tusk is used. It could be a **spear** to catch food. Or a **weapon.** Or just an **ornament.**

Narwhal

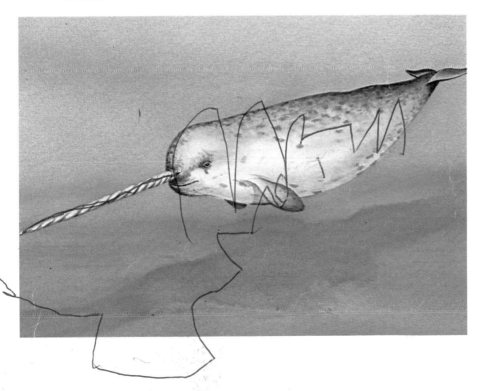

Except for the sperm whale or **cachalot** (KASH-a-lot), toothed whales are smaller than baleen whales. Many of them are less than 15 feet (4.5 m) long. **Dolphins** (DOLL-fins) and **porpoises** (PORE-pusses) are members of the toothed whale family. The porpoise is one of the smallest members. It usually measures less than 6 feet (1.8 m) in length.

Porpoise skimming surface of the water

Dolphins are thought to be very intelligent. In captivity, they have been trained to do tricks. They have also been trained to carry equipment to sea divers.

The **bottlenose dolphin** is the best-known dolphin. It is the one most often seen in **aquariums** (a-KWER-e-ums). It is about 9 feet (2.7 m) long. It has a dark back, a white belly, and a short **snout** (nose). Everyone likes to watch dolphins do their tricks.

The **killer** or **grampus** (GRAM-pus) whale and the **pilot whale** are also toothed whales. The killer whale is strong and intelligent. And it is the fastest swimming whale in the world. It can travel at speeds of up to 30 knots (34.5 miles or 55.6 km per hour). The killer whale is the only whale that preys on mammals. It eats seals, porpoises, and even small whales. Killer whales are sometimes called **"sea wolves."**

Killer whales travel and hunt together in packs.

Killer whales performing at the Miami Seaquarium

Killer whales are sometimes kept in **captivity.** When in captivity, they are easily tamed. They even become very friendly toward their keepers.

The sperm whale is the giant of the toothed whales. The largest grow up to 60 feet (18 m) long. They feed on giant squid and dive deep to find them.

Sperm whale feeding on squid

A sperm whale is easy to recognize. It has a
massive, blunt-shaped head, unlike any other
whale. Only the lower jaw has teeth, but they are
very big! Each tooth is 10 inches (25 cm) long and
weighs about 2 pounds (1 kg). Inside the head is a
large store of oil, called **spermaceti**
(spur-ma-SET-ee). It was once used to make
candles, soap, and cosmetics.

A large sperm whale might have ½ ton of spermaceti. People hunt sperm whales for **ambergris** (AM-burr-grays). Ambergris comes from the **intestines** of the sperm whale. It is used to make expensive **perfumes.**

Whalers with a very large chunk of ambergris. This piece weighed 155 pounds (70 kg). Usually, ambergris weighs about 20 pounds (10 kg).

Lamplighters in the early 1800s

Whaling (hunting whales) was once an important industry. People went to sea in **whalers** (large boats) to hunt the whale. They wanted it mainly for its blubber, baleen, and meat. Blubber can be melted down into oil. Before electricity, whale oil was used for lighting lamps.

Baleen, or **whalebone,** was used to stiffen collars and ladies' **corsets.** Today, **plastic** is used to do these same things. Whale meat is eaten by some people. It is also used to make pet foods.

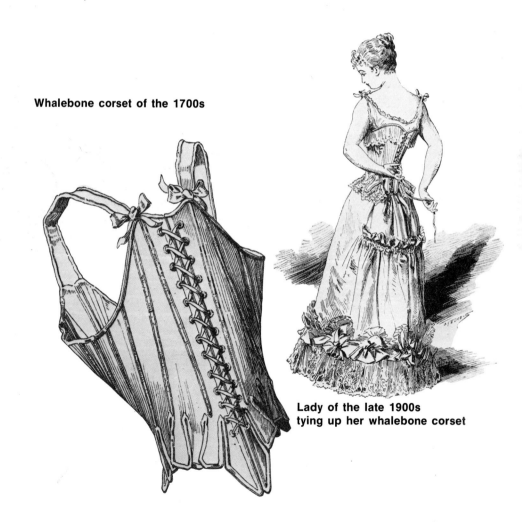

Whalebone corset of the 1700s

Lady of the late 1900s
tying up her whalebone corset

Eskimos preparing for a whale hunt

Many **Eskimos** (ES-ka-mos) still depend on whales for their living. They have hunted them for many hundreds of years. Eskimos catch the whale for its meat and oil. They use parts of its body to make tools and clothes.

Countries that hunt whales are called **whaling nations.** Today, the **Soviet Union** and **Japan** are the most active whaling nations. The **International Whaling Commission** is a group of people from 19 whaling nations. They meet each year to talk about hunting whales. They make rules limiting the numbers and species that may be killed. They are trying to keep whales from dying out.

A modern Russian whaler (whaling boat). It has two huge decks. Each deck is as large as a football field.

Fin whale being cut up at a whaling station

There used to be large numbers of whales in the world. Then, too many were killed. The Greenland right whale, or **bowhead,** almost died out. Large numbers of blue whales were also destroyed. There are only a few thousand still alive. Today, many kinds are in danger of becoming **extinct** (disappearing). So laws are necessary to protect them.

Great blue whales are now totally protected. People are no longer allowed to hunt them. Some people **(conservationists)** would like all whales protected from hunters. They believe whales have a right to live out their natural lives. And humans should not take away that right.

Ship belonging to the Greenpeace Movement, a group of conservationists. These conservationists try to keep whales from being caught.

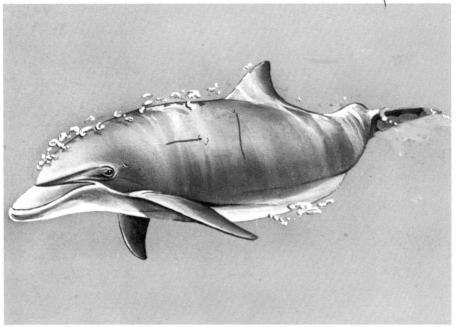

Bottlenosed dolphin

Scientists still have many questions about whales. Why do whales sing? How do they speak to each other? And what do they say? Are whales more intelligent than humans? What can we learn from them? Perhaps some day we will have the answers to these questions. But only if whales are allowed to survive.

INDEX